A FIRST LOOK AT POISONOUS SNAKES

By Millicent E. Selsam and Joyce Hunt

Illustrated by Harriett Springer

WALKER AND COMPANY ✸ NEW YORK

First published in the United States of America in 1987 by the Walker Publishing Company, Inc.

Published simultaneously in Canada by John Wiley & Sons Canada, Limited, Rexdale, Ontario.

Library of Congress Cataloging-in-Publication Data

Selsam, Millicent Ellis, 1912-
   A first look at poisonous snakes.

   (A First look at series)
   Summary: Describes the physical characteristics and habitat of several different poisonous snakes and their benefits to man.
      1. Poisonous snakes--Juvenile literature.
[1. Poisonous snakes. 2. Snakes] I. Hunt, Joyce.
II. Springer, Harriett, ill. III. Title. IV. Series:
Selsam, Millicent Ellis, 1912-   . First look at
series.
QL666.O6S392 1987   597.96'0469   86-33979
ISBN 0-8027-6681-1
ISBN 0-8027-6683-8 (lib. bdg.)

Printed in the United States of America

10 9 8 7 6 5 4 3 2 1

A *FIRST LOOK AT* SERIES

Each of the nature books in this series is planned to develop the child's powers of observation—to train him or her to notice distinguishing charteristics. A leaf is a leaf. A bird is a bird. An insect is an insect. That is true. But what makes an oak leaf different from a maple leaf? Why is a hawk different from an eagle, or a beetle different from a bug?

Classification is a painstaking science. These books give a child the essence of the search for differences that is the basis for scientific classification.

For Jessica

Many people are afraid of snakes. Are you?
There are about 2500 different kinds of snakes in the world.
But only about 300 are poisonous.
It is a good idea to learn to recognize the
poisonous ones that may live where you live.

Poisonous snakes have 2 hollow needle-like teeth
called fangs.
The fangs of one kind are short and cannot move.
Cobras belong in this group.

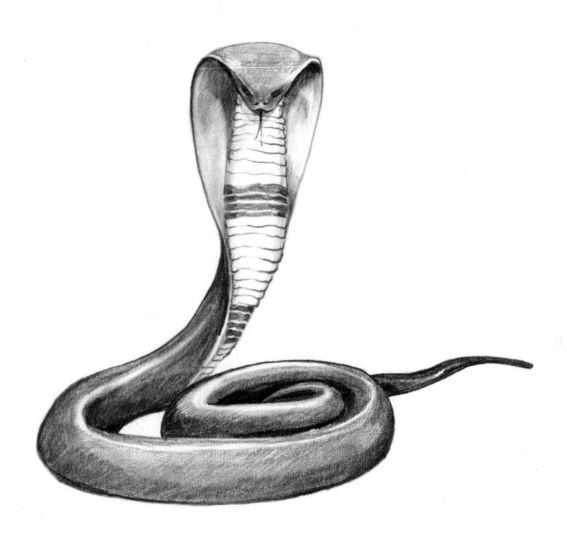

The fangs of another kind are long and fold back in the snake's mouth.
Rattlesnakes belong in this group.

COBRAS AND THEIR RELATIVES

Many cobras have hoods of loose skin that cover long
rib bones.
The hood spreads open like an umbrella when the snake
is disturbed.
This makes the snake look bigger and helps to scare its
enemies away.

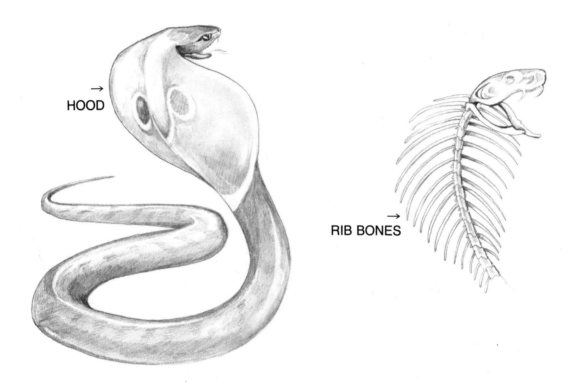

HOOD

RIB BONES

Cobras live in Asia and Africa.

There are different kinds of cobras.
The King Cobra is four times bigger than the Indian Cobra.
Which is which?

Look at the markings on the back of the Indian
Cobra's neck.
They look like eyeglasses.
Not all cobras have these markings.

This cobra can be told by its markings.
It is called a Black-Necked Cobra.

The Black-Necked Cobra spits its poison into the
eyes of any person or animal that tries to attack it.

The Mamba, a relative of the cobra,
is one of the most dangerous snakes in Africa.
It has a long, thin body and can climb trees and
move at great speed.
There are two kinds of Mambas, a black one and
a green one. The Black Mamba is the most dangerous.

The Coral Snake is also a relative of the cobra.
It lives in North and South America.
This small snake has bands of color around its body.

VIPER SNAKES AND THEIR RELATIVES

The hollow fangs of the vipers are so long that
they must be folded back when the snake closes its mouth.
The poison is made in a sac in its head.
From there it runs down through a tube into the fangs.

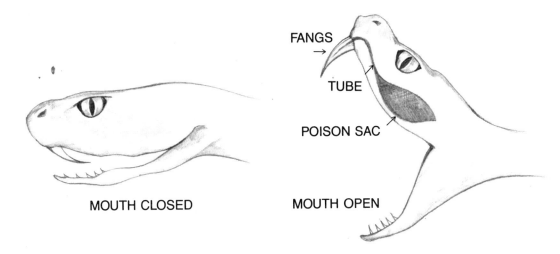

MOUTH CLOSED   MOUTH OPEN

The large poison sac makes the heads of vipers look
V shaped.

Vipers have heavy bodies and usually lie very still and wait for their prey to pass by.

There are two kinds of vipers.
Some have pits. Some do not have pits.
The pits are two small holes, one on each side of
the head. The pits sense body heat from warm-blooded
prey. This helps the snake to aim when it strikes.

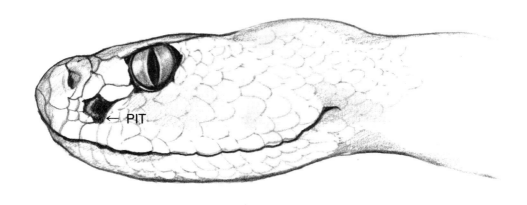

← PIT

PIT VIPERS

Most of the Pit Vipers live in North and South America. The most well known are the rattlesnakes. Rattlesnakes are the only snakes with horny buttons called rattles. A new one grows at the end of its tail each time the snake sheds its skin. Rattlesnakes usually shed their skins two or three times a year.

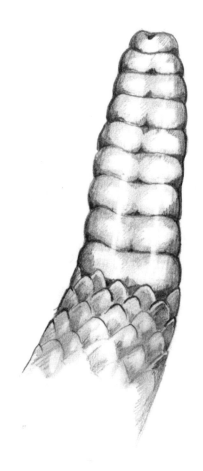

You can tell some rattlesnakes apart by their size. Four or five little Pygmy Rattlesnakes are as big as one Eastern Diamondback Rattlesnake.

Sometimes the markings are a clue that helps tell one rattlesnake from another.

Find the rattlesnake with diamond shaped markings.
Find the one with a black tail.
Find the one with dark bands around its pale body.

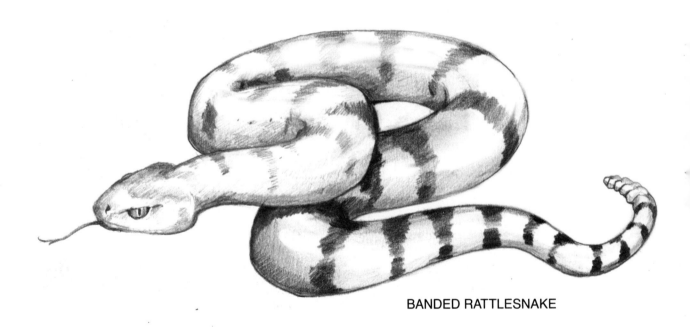

BANDED RATTLESNAKE

ROCK RATTLESNAKE

WESTERN DIAMONDBACK RATTLESNAKE

Here's the "rock and roll" star of the snake world.
It rocks and rolls as it moves from side to side in the sand.
It is called a Sidewinder.
Where it has passed by you can see S shaped loops.

Cottonmouths and Copperheads are not rattlesnakes
but they are pit vipers.
Look for the Cottonmouth.
When it is disturbed it opens its mouth wide.
The inside is as white as cotton.
Look for the Copperhead.
It has hourglass markings.

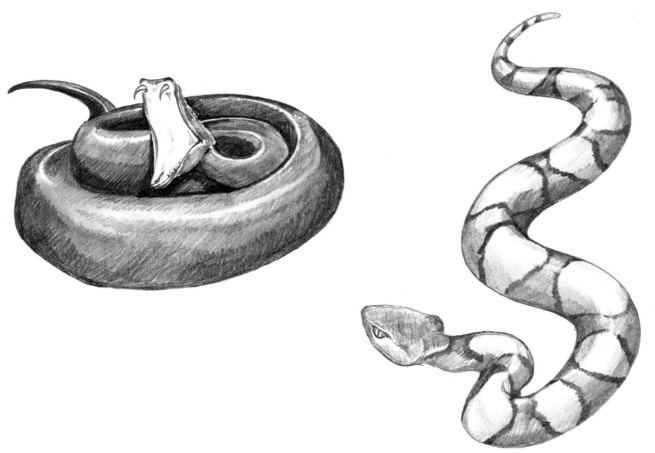

VIPERS WITHOUT PITS

Most of the vipers without pits live in Europe,
Asia, and Africa.
You can tell these two vipers apart by their markings.

Which viper has a dark V behind its head?
Which viper has egg shaped spots?

RUSSEL'S VIPER

EUROPEAN VIPER

24

These two vipers have "horns."
Which viper has horns over its eyes?
Which viper has horns on its nose?

HORNED VIPER

RHINOCEROS VIPER

SEA SNAKES

Did you know that there are snakes that live
in the sea?
All of them are poisonous.
Many have bodies that are flat, not round.
Their tails look like paddles.
They live in the Pacific and Indian Oceans.

Are poisonous snakes of any use to people?
Yes. Many snakes, even poisonous ones
destroy rats and mice.
Some eat harmful insects.
Some eat other small animals that eat crops.
Also the poison, or venom, may be used by doctors
in medical research.
Venom is also used to make antivenom (*an*-tie-ven-om).
The antivenom is used to treat people and animals
bitten by poisonous snakes.

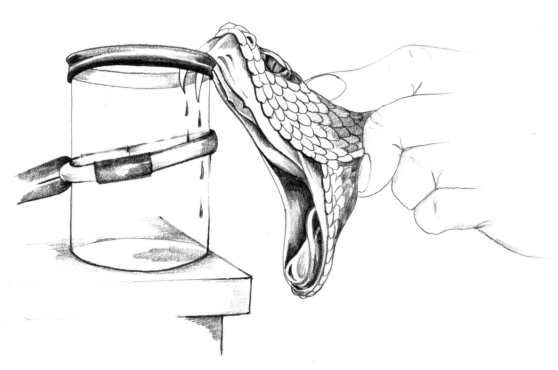

SCIENTIST TAKING THE VENOM FROM THE FANGS OF A POISONOUS SNAKE.

PARTS OF THE WORLD WHERE POISONOUS SNAKES LIVE

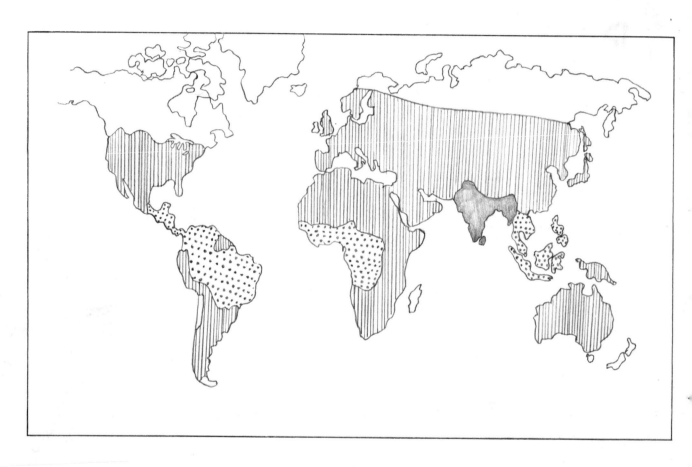

NO DANGER

VERY LITTLE DANGER

SOME DANGER

DANGER!

TO AVOID BEING BITTEN BY POISONOUS SNAKES:

Read about them and find out where they live.

If you are in poisonous snake country:
Be sure to wear heavy high boots,

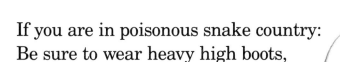

If you see ANY snake, back away quickly and carefully,
Don't try to find out if it is poisonous.

Do not sleep on the ground without a tent.

Look ahead before you climb.
Never put your hand or foot in a place you can't see.

TO TELL POISONOUS SNAKES APART:

Look for hoods.

Look for rattles.

Look at the size.

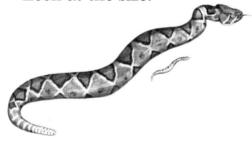

Look at their markings.

Look at their shape.

Look for snakes that spit.

Look at the way it moves.

Look for horns.

POISONOUS SNAKES IN THIS BOOK: